— THE UNTOLD STORY OF —

A. PHILIP RANDOLPH

UNION ORGANIZER AND CIVIL RIGHTS ACTIVIST

BY DR. ARTIKA R. TYNER

Consultant:
Dr. Clarence Lang
Susan Welch Dean of the College of the Liberal Arts
Professor of African American Studies
The Pennsylvania State University

CAPSTONE PRESS
a capstone imprint

Published by Capstone Press, an imprint of Capstone
1710 Roe Crest Drive, North Mankato, Minnesota 56003
capstonepub.com

Library of Congress Cataloging-in-Publication Data is available on the Library of Congress website.

ISBN: 9781669069959 (hardcover)
ISBN: 9781669069904 (paperback)
ISBN: 9781669069911 (ebook PDF)

Summary: You may have heard about labor organizers like Cesar Chavez, who helped organize farmworkers in California. But decades earlier, A. Philip Randolph started a union for Black porters who worked on Pullman railcars. It was the first mostly Black union in the United States. Randolph was also involved in the Civil Rights Movement and helped organize the March on Washington in 1963. Uncover Randolph's story and his important work as a labor organizer and civil rights activist.

Editorial Credits
Editor: Ericka Smith; Designer: Sarah Bennett; Media Researcher: Svetlana Zhurkin; Production Specialist: Katy LaVigne

Image Credits
Collection of the Smithsonian National Museum of African American History and Culture: 15; DVIC: NARA/E.F. Joseph, 21; Getty Images: Hulton Archive, 17, 29, Hulton Archive/Keystone/Vince Finnigan, 23, Hulton Archive/MPI, 24; Library of Congress: cover, 9 (bottom), 13, 18, 19, 20; The New York Public Library: General Research Division, 10, Schomburg Center for Research in Black Culture/Jean Blackwell Hutson Research and Reference Division, 7, Schomburg Center for Research in Black Culture/Manuscripts, Archives and Rare Books Division, 11, The Miriam and Ira D. Wallach Division of Art/Prints and Photographs/Picture Collection, 9 (top); Newscom: Everett Collection, 5, 25, 26; Shutterstock: Everett Collection, 16, Julia Khimich (background), cover (right) and throughout, Nadegda Rozova (background), cover (left) and throughout, spatuletail, 27

Printed and bound in the USA. 5853

TABLE OF CONTENTS

Words in **bold** are in the glossary.

CHANGE FOR BLACK WORKERS

After slavery was **abolished** in the United States, many Black people struggled to find meaningful employment. But in the late 1800s, one business was one of the largest employers for Black men—the Pullman Company. Black men worked as **porters** on Pullman railcars. They served passengers. They also maintained the trains.

In 1925, the porters were tired of dangerous working conditions and low wages. They wanted change. They asked the labor **organizer** A. Philip Randolph to speak at a meeting. This was the beginning of the first mostly Black labor union— the International Brotherhood of Sleeping Car Porters and Maids (BSCP).

Randolph proved himself to be a skilled organizer. He also played a key role in the Civil Rights Movement. He helped organize the 1963 March on Washington for Jobs and Freedom.

Many people know about the 1960s farmworker organizer Cesar Chavez. But there was a lot of labor organizing happening in the first half of the 20th century that people don't know about—like Randolph's work. This is his story.

CHAPTER ONE

ORGANIZING WORKERS

Asa Philip Randolph was born on April 15, 1889. He was born in Crescent City, Florida. His parents were James William and Elizabeth Robinson Randolph. His father was a minister. His mother was a seamstress. He was the younger of two sons.

Randolph's parents prioritized education. They also told him about people who fought against slavery, like Nat Turner and Frederick Douglass. They taught their son to take a stand for Black liberation.

In 1907, Randolph went to Cookman Institute. It was the first educational institution for Black people in Florida. He graduated at the top of his class.

Cookman Institute in 1922

In 1911, Randolph moved to Harlem. He worked during the day as a **switchboard operator**. He also took classes at City College. He studied economics, history, philosophy, and politics. He also started trying to organize workers.

In 1914, he started working for an employment agency. It was called the Brotherhood of Labor. He wanted to help Black people access jobs with good pay.

That same year, Randolph married Lucille Green. Green was a wealthy entrepreneur who owned a beauty salon. She supported Randolph's work financially. She also motivated him to keep fighting for justice.

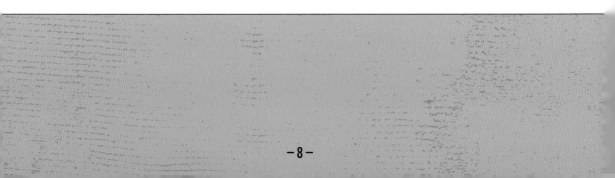

City College in the early 1900s

FACT Randolph was inspired to fight for racial justice by W.E.B. Du Bois. In 1903, Dr. Du Bois wrote *The Souls of Black Folk*, which outlined challenges facing the Black community and ways to achieve equal justice.

When the United States entered World War I in 1917, Randolph advocated for Black people to have access to military jobs. This would provide opportunities for education and career development.

In 1917, Randolph and his friend Chandler Owen founded the magazine the *Messenger*. It introduced Black people to **socialist** ideas that focused on building unity, protecting the dignity of work, and organizing labor unions. The magazine encouraged readers to become more active in politics too.

The *Messenger* grew in popularity. It was an essential guide for Black workers. It became the third most popular magazine after the *Crisis*, the magazine of the National Association for the Advancement of Colored People (NAACP), and *Opportunity*, a popular magazine during the **Harlem Renaissance.**

A. Philip Randolph   Chandler Owen

FACT Between about 1916 and 1970, nearly 6 million Black people moved from the South to cities in the North and the West, like Chicago, Detroit, and New York City. Many organizations developed to address their economic, social, and political needs and interests.

ORGANIZING FOR JUSTICE

When the Pullman porters invited Randolph to speak in June 1925, they wanted to see a change in their working conditions. Many worked 100 hours per week. They had little time for rest. They also did not have opportunities for promotions. Better roles like serving as a conductor were only given to white men. Black women working on trains faced similar challenges. They served as underpaid maids and attendants.

To address these problems, the porters wanted to organize a union. Randolph was invited to tell them how to build their union.

After this meeting, the porters asked Randolph to lead their organization—what would soon be named the International Brotherhood of Sleeping Car Porters and Maids. Later it became known as just the Brotherhood of Sleeping Car Porters.

Working as a Pullman Porter

Chicago businessman George Pullman hired the first Pullman porter for his railcars around 1867. He believed previously enslaved Black men would know how to serve white passengers. By the 1920s, the Pullman Company was the largest employer of Black people in the United States.

All of the porters were called "George" no matter what their actual names were. This reflected a practice during slavery. Enslaved people were called by the names of their masters.

Pullman also overworked the porters and paid them low wages. They were required to work 400 hours a month, and they relied on tips to make a living.

A Pullman porter in the late 1800s

At the time, Black workers were not allowed to join other labor unions. The meeting in 1925 marked the beginning of the country's first mostly Black labor union.

On August 25, 1925, Randolph spoke to a large group of porters about unionizing. During his speech, Randolph shared with them a vision of brotherhood. He described the porters as a group with a common purpose. He said they had a responsibility to protect one another. He also prepared the porters for the fear and intimidation they would face. The men courageously agreed to take action.

Black women also played an important role in establishing the union. Women were not usually seen as union members. Because of that misconception, Black women were able to organize and build the union across the country.

> **FACT** Rosina Corrothers Tucker, the wife of a porter, was an organizer for BSCP. She helped convince porters to join the union, collected dues, and conveyed information between union members.

A Pullman porter named T.R. Joseph in the 1930s

Randolph fundraised and traveled around the country to set up chapters of the union in different cities, including Chicago, St. Louis, and Oakland.

In 1935, BSCP was recognized by the American Federation of Labor (AFL). It was the first mostly Black labor union to become a member of the AFL. This was an opportunity to connect labor rights with the fight for racial justice.

Randolph also led negotiations with the Pullman Company. Once, the company sent him a signed blank check, hoping to **bribe** him. He was encouraged to write in an amount up to $1 million. But Randolph didn't take the bribe. He wrote that he would not be silenced whenever there was an injustice—no matter how much money he was offered.

Pullman porters celebrating the 11th anniversary of the union in New York City in 1936

Standing Up for Farmworkers

In 1962, Cesar Chavez helped found the National Farm Workers Association (now known as United Farm Workers) in California. Farmworkers in the area were underpaid, overworked, and exposed to hazardous chemicals.

Chavez and other organizers used nonviolent resistance to advocate for better pay and working conditions. In 1965, they organized a strike against grape growers in San Joaquin Valley. In 1966, Chavez led a 340-mile (547-kilometer) march from Delano to California's capitol building in Sacramento. And in 1968, he fasted for 25 days in support of grape workers.

These strategies earned the movement a lot of attention. The strike even earned support from Dr. Martin Luther King Jr. and Robert F. Kennedy. Finally, in 1970, the grape workers negotiated a new contract with grape growers.

Chavez continued advocating for farmworkers' right to a fair salary and a safe workplace until he died in 1993. He has become one of the most iconic labor organizers of the 20th century.

Randolph supported other efforts to help Black workers too. In 1936, he helped establish the National Negro Congress (NNC). It brought together religious, civil rights, political, and labor groups. They were concerned about how the Great Depression (1929–1941) limited economic opportunities for Black people. They also wanted to see an end to police brutality, lynchings, and housing discrimination. The NNC also helped the Congress of Industrial Organizations (CIO) organize Black and white workers in the auto, steel, and meatpacking industries.

Housing in a Black neighborhood in Atlanta, Georgia, in 1936

A Pullman porter taking a break aboard a train in 1942

On April 25, 1937—after 12 years of organizing—
Randolph successfully negotiated the Pullman porters'
first contract. They won better wages and reduced
hours. Porters received their largest pay increase
ever. Their work hours were limited to 240 hours per
month. And they were guaranteed time to rest.

Randolph in 1942

When the United States started producing materials for World War II (1939–1945), Randolph saw a missed opportunity for Black workers. He wanted Black people to access work in factories. He decided to plan a march on Washington, DC, to end **segregation** in war industries.

On January 25, 1941, Randolph announced the march. The NAACP, the National Urban League, and Black fraternities and sororities joined his efforts. Initially, Randolph said 10,000 protesters would participate. He later promised 100,000 participants.

This threat scared President Franklin D. Roosevelt. On June 25, 1941, he issued Executive Order 8802. It prohibited racial segregation in war industries. Millions of Black men and women gained access to good jobs.

A Black woman helps build a military ship in California in 1943.

WORKING TOWARD EQUAL RIGHTS

After World War II, Randolph still had work to do. In 1945, he created what would become the League for Nonviolent Civil Disobedience Against Military Segregation. In just a few years, the organization had convinced President Harry Truman to end segregation in the U.S. military. On July 26, 1948, Truman issued Executive Order 9981, desegregating the country's armed forces.

Throughout the 1950s and 1960s, Randolph continued his work of creating equal access to jobs. He also taught leaders of the Civil Rights Movement how to organize protests and use the principles of nonviolent resistance. He trained and inspired leaders like Dr. Martin Luther King Jr. and Bayard Rustin.

Randolph (center right) next to King (center left)
speaking to journalists in 1958

Randolph also decided to organize another march on Washington, DC, to support civil rights legislation. He worked with other organizations, including the NAACP, the National Urban League, the Congress of Racial Equality (CORE), the Southern Christian Leadership Conference (SCLC), the Student Nonviolent Coordinating Committee (SNCC), the National Council of Churches, and United Auto Workers (UAW).

The March on Washington for Jobs and Freedom took place on August 28, 1963. About 250,000 people gathered at the Lincoln Memorial. Randolph gave the opening speech. Dr. Martin Luther King Jr. gave his famous "I Have a Dream" speech.

Randolph (second from right) and other leaders during the March on Washington for Jobs and Freedom

The march convinced Congress and the president to act. It helped lead to the Civil Rights Act of 1964 and the Voting Rights Act of 1965. These acts challenged segregation in public spaces, outlawed employment discrimination, and got rid of things like **poll taxes** that kept Black people from voting.

Bayard Rustin

Bayard Rustin was a well-trained and dedicated community organizer. His grandparents taught him about achieving peace, unity, and harmony through nonviolence. He traveled to India and studied Mahatma Gandhi's strategies.

Rustin organized campaigns for civil rights organizations. He advised Dr. King during the Montgomery Bus Boycott. And he was the lead organizer of the March on Washington for Jobs and Freedom.

Rustin (left) with another march organizer on August 13, 1963

LABOR RIGHTS ARE HUMAN RIGHTS

Randolph remained an advocate even later in life. In 1965, he founded the A. Philip Randolph Institute with Rustin. They wanted all workers to experience justice in three key areas—economic, political, and social.

Randolph with President Johnson in 1968

In 1966, Randolph released "A Freedom Budget for All Americans." This $185 billion blueprint for economic justice identified ways to end poverty. It focused on access to jobs, a good education, healthcare, and stable housing.

Randolph continued to train and mentor emerging civil rights leaders until 1968. That year, he resigned from his leadership position due to health issues and retired from public life. He passed away in 1979. He was 90 years old.

A U.S. postal stamp honored Randolph and his work in 1989.

Today, the Black community still faces economic injustice. Research shows that it will take more than 200 years to end the **racial wealth gap**. This is a result of persistent employment discrimination, low wages, limited educational opportunities, and a lack of business resources.

But Randolph's legacy still has an impact today. He inspired future generations of leaders who are making a difference in their communities. John Hope Bryant, for example, founded Operation HOPE to provide financial education, promote job creation, and support wealth building. Others are organizing protests, running for political office, and creating businesses. Their efforts are helping advance Randolph's vision of economic justice and freedom.

Randolph in 1950

GLOSSARY

abolish (uh-BOL-ish)—to put an end to something

bribe (BRIBE)—money or gifts used to persuade someone to do something, especially something illegal or dishonest

Harlem Renaissance (HAR-luhm REN-uh-sahnss)—a time of increased creation of and interest in Black art from the late 1910s to the late 1930s, centered in the New York City neighborhood of Harlem

organizer (OR-guh-nye-zuhr)—a person who gets people to join an organization

poll tax (POHL TAKS)—a fee someone must pay in order to vote

porter (POR-tur)—a person who works on a train and provides services

racial wealth gap (RAY-shuhl WELTH GAP)—the amount of wealth compared across racial groups

segregation (seg-ruh-GAY-shuhn)—the practice of keeping groups of people apart, especially based on race

socialist (SOH-shuh-lihst)—related to an economic system in which the community controls the means of producing and distributing goods, usually through the government

switchboard operator (SWICH-bord OP-er-ay-tuhr)—a person who connects the lines of a telephone system so that people can make telephone calls

READ MORE

Miller, J.P. *Bayard Rustin*. Vero Beach, FL: Rourke Educational Media, 2021.

Oxtra, Cristina. *The Untold Story of Larry Itliong: Labor Rights Hero*. North Mankato, MN: Capstone, 2023.

Weston, Margeaux. *The March on Washington: A Day That Changed America*. North Mankato, MN: Capstone, 2022.

INTERNET SITES

Britannica Kids: A. Philip Randolph
kids.britannica.com/kids/article/A-Philip-Randolph/628644

National Geographic Kids: 1963 March on Washington
kids.nationalgeographic.com/history/article/march-on-washington

Zinn Education Project: Jan. 25 1941: A Philip Randolph and March on Washington
zinnedproject.org/news/tdih/a-philip-randolph-first-call-mow

INDEX

ABOUT THE AUTHOR

Dr. Artika R. Tyner is a passionate educator,
award-winning author, civil rights attorney,
sought-after speaker, and advocate for justice.
She lives in Saint Paul, Minnesota, and is the
founder of the Planting People Growing Justice
Leadership Institute.